FIVE PRINCIPLES FOR THE POSITIVE PRACTICE OF LAW:
The Essential Guide to Success as a New Lawyer

By
Victoria Cecil Walker, Esq.

www.5principlesbook.com

ISBN: 978-0-615-44176-4

This book is dedicated to the Honorable Justice
Harry Lee Anstead
and the Honorable Justice Ricky L. Polston
of the Supreme Court of the State of Florida –
Two gentlemen whom I believe exemplify
the five principles.

It is indeed a sacred trust to practice law and uphold the tenets of our noble profession. Our legal education is a gift, and it enables us to make our livings with our minds, to explore and pursue justice in all of its varied forms, and to resolve conflict in a peaceful, civilized, and courteous manner. The gifts of our education and professional oath require each and every one of us to work by the highest standards of honesty, integrity, and fairness to ensure equal justice for all. We lawyers are held to higher standards because we chose them to apply to us, and because we drive the wheels of justice.

-- Mayanne Downs
President of The Florida Bar
2010-2011

TABLE OF CONTENTS

INTRODUCTION 1

CHAPTER ONE 5

History 5

CHAPTER TWO 11

Competency 11

CHAPTER THREE 17

Humility 17

CHAPTER FOUR 23

Integrity 23

CHAPTER FIVE 27

Credibility 27

CONCLUSION 31

Bibliography 33

INTRODUCTION

This book is about perspective. How often have we learned that goals are achieved a lot easier when we pursue them with the right perspective? Now apply this lesson to the practice of law: Practicing law with the right perspective will truly yield positive results in a profession that is largely negative in nature.

Several studies show that lawyers suffer much higher incidents of depression than the general population. According to a study by Johns Hopkins University, lawyers ranked first among 28 occupations studied in the rate of clinical depression. Also, according to a report published by the National Institute of Occupational Safety and Health in the early 1990's, male lawyers in the United States are two times more likely to commit suicide than men in the general population. The reasons for the high depression rate are believed to be largely based on the negative nature of the legal profession. For instance, the profession itself is inherently conflict-driven, involving high stakes, i.e. loss of property, life or freedom, frequently in an "all or nothing" environment. Also, the culture of most law firms is very hierarchical and competitive, the lawyer's work is under constant scrutiny from his peers and the courts, and lawyers are taught to anticipate the negative and aim for perfection. Furthermore, lawyers are often repeatedly exposed to negative behavior, especially in the areas of criminal and family law. Prior to law school, many law students have no exposure to the daily life of a lawyer.

My hope is that this book will change your approach to the practice of law by transforming your perspective on the practice itself and becoming more aware of the important role you play in society. During my sixteen-year career in the legal profession, employed in every capacity from file clerk to paralegal to an

1

attorney, working in law firms and the state court system, I found that the most stable lawyers, both mentally and spiritually, possessed five basic characteristics. I've concluded that these basic principles are essential not only to the practice of law itself, but also to a more positive experience in the profession. I don't profess to be an expert on psychology or human behavior, but I do believe practicing these principles will bring you success in your legal career. Not success in terms of material wealth - although such a result could occur - but rather success in terms of true happiness and satisfaction.

• The five principles begin with an awareness of **history** and the importance of maintaining that historical perspective in your practice. Having an awareness of the role lawyers played in society in past centuries inspires us to do better in the present.

• The second principle is **competency**. Being competent is more than just possessing a law degree. It is exercising the skills learned in law school in the right context, with the right attitude, and with a dose of practicality.

• Third, you must practice law with a sense of **humility.** Being humble is not a weakness, but is a strength of great magnitude. Humility is about serving others with quiet confidence and without self-inflation.

• The fourth principle is **integrity**, which is sometimes described as doing the right thing when no one is looking. It is really best understood through example. Since appearing in print in 1960, the famous protagonist in Harper Lee's *To Kill a Mockingbird,* Atticus Finch, has served as a model of integrity for all lawyers and by his example has inspired many to join the profession. The path to the positive practice of law is truly paved with integrity.

•   The last principle is **credibility**. In a profession where the prime objective is truth, credibility is everything. If you are not perceived as trustworthy, your legal career will be short and not so sweet.

It is my belief that this quick read will give you the solid foundation you need to build your positive practice of law and find true fulfillment in your legal career.

Elitess Maximus, Attorney at Law

CHAPTER ONE

History

You have to know the past to understand the present.

~ Dr. Carl Sagan

It has been said that having an awareness of history makes us strive to do better. Not surprisingly, history shows that the lawyer has been generally disliked for centuries. This is probably the reason why the history of the profession is not taught in law schools in any great detail. Nevertheless, it is important to know this history, for understanding how lawyers were viewed in the past will provide the foundation on which to build a more positive law practice in the present. Like many professions, the legal profession evolved out of necessity. There are many great books available that provide a detailed account of the legal profession from its inception in ancient times to today. This chapter will provide just a brief synopsis of this history and possible reasons for the decline in the way the profession is regarded.

In ancient times, "law" was primarily religious and thus was thought to be divinely inspired. Therefore, legal issues were decided by astrologers, priests, prophets, kings, or judges. However, as the world grew larger and more diverse, the law became more secularized and eventually codified for easier application to the masses. Over time the law changed from being primarily religious to standard codes based on right and wrong. Eventually, the law was split into two categories: public and private.

Public offenses affected the community as a whole, such as treason, desertion from the military, and embezzlement of public funds. In such cases, any private citizen could act as the prosecutor against the accused. If the accused was convicted, the prosecutor may receive a portion of the imposed fine or the defendant's property if confiscated. Cases were initially heard by a magistrate or judge. If it was determined that a legitimate dispute existed, and neither a verdict nor settlement between the parties could be reached, the case was transferred to the court for trial by jury.

In private cases, only the person affected by the alleged claim could act as the prosecutor. Unlike public cases, private cases were brought before an arbitrator who was chosen from a roster of citizens and paid a small fee by the prosecutor. The arbitrator would report his decision to the magistrate who assigned him the case, which could be appealed to the courts by the losing party.

In cases accepted for trial, sworn statements were taken from witnesses and were read aloud in court. No new evidence could be presented and no cross-examination was allowed. The parties addressed the jury directly and the jury decided the cases immediately after the hearing. In all cases, each party acted as their own lawyer with the exception of homicide cases, in which a relative of the deceased would act as prosecutor. All citizens, with the exception of women, children and the infirm, were expected to defend themselves. If a person did appear on a party's behalf, it was usually an interested friend. This system seemed to work for several centuries.

As legal issues grew more complex, so did juries' appreciation for good case presentation. Eventually, litigants would secretly retain speech writers who were well versed in the law to prepare a speech about the case that the litigant could read aloud in court. Ultimately, good oratory skills became necessary as philosophical thinking and social and political issues became more complex. As a result, society was more receptive to the idea of having someone other than the litigant speak in court on a litigant's behalf. At the time, the preferred method of advocacy generally involved circumstantial reasoning and sound logical argument with little reliance on direct evidence. There was a belief that direct evidence was not trustworthy because it could be faked, modified, or someone could be bribed. Hence, the practice of rhetoric became a desired skill in legal advocacy. Consequently, from the speech writer and orator, the "advocate" (or lawyer) was born.

At first, these "advocates" were trained only in rhetoric, not law, and they were prohibited by law from taking a fee to plead a case on behalf of another. However, as the need for such representation grew, this prohibition was widely ignored. By the late Fourth Century, courses of legal study were being offered and advocates were studying law in addition to rhetoric. However, it was not until the Thirteenth Century that attempts to regulate this "profession" were made in some parts of Europe, the first being a mandate that all lawyers swear an oath of admission before practicing in the courts.

Naturally, as the world faced economic and demographic expansion, more disputes would arise that needed expedient and consistent resolution. Although the demand for lawyers to resolve these disputes increased, formal institutional training of lawyers was not required until the Nineteenth Century. Until then, most people entered the legal profession through reading the law or some form of apprenticeship.

In this country, the early colonists were unreceptive to lawyers; this distrust arose from several sources. First, colonists associated lawyers with government, and after being oppressed by the English government, this association naturally had an adverse effect on the profession. As a result, colonists preferred to manage their affairs and business dealings on their own without third party assistance. Second, in addition to being associated with government, lawyers were associated with the upper class. (Interestingly, it has been said that the upper class often questioned the lawyers' loyalty and was even intimidated by their perceived power and influence.) Nevertheless, this association essentially alienated the lawyer from the average colonist. Finally, the adversarial system in which the lawyer practiced was unpopular among the theocratic colonists, such as the Quakers. The legal profession with its formalities and unique language seemed incompatible with the simple and amicable system they sought. The lawyer was viewed as too harsh and contentious.

Despite this hostility, as long as society presented problems for which lawyers had an answer the profession thrived, especially as the country pushed farther West. In some Western states, lawyers were particularly needed to establish legal systems not yet in existence. Property and water rights became more prevalent and the onset of the Industrial Revolution spawned more labor and employment disputes. Thus, as civilization grew more dense and commercial, legal skills and services became essential. However, with such a demand for legal services came increased complaints of incompetent lawyers who were careless in their work and greedy lawyers who were accused of inciting frivolous lawsuits for profit. Naturally, the onslaught of untrained and unfettered lawyers perpetuated society's discontentment for the profession. Moreover, as the country grew, lawyers developed an association with politics which, for obvious reasons, did not improve public opinion about the profession.

In response, professional bar associations were established in each state, the first informally in Mississippi in 1821. One hundred years later, the first mandatory bar was established by legislative action in North Dakota in 1921. Initially, these associations were mainly exclusive social organizations of elite lawyers. Over time, however, state bar associations became more inclusive and eventually undertook a more regulatory and disciplinary role for the profession. To this day, state bar associations work feverishly to impose and enforce rules designed to maintain the integrity of the legal profession. Yet, despite its efforts, society continues to view lawyers as dishonest shysters trying to make a fast buck.

Nevertheless, our system of government, and indeed our system of law, would not have come to pass if it wasn't for the work of lawyers. This system was built in large part from lawyers serving others in the form of representation in thousands of cases which produced judicial decisions that affected the law. The lawyers who built our system from the ground up believed in it so deeply that they risked their lives and sacrificed their livelihood by penning their names on the declaration that birthed our nation. (Out of the 56 individuals who signed the Declaration of Independence, 24 were lawyers.) And because of the ongoing work of lawyers, this system has survived for more than two centuries.

One important thing to keep in mind is that regardless of society's distrust of lawyers over the centuries, the lawyer's role as "peacemaker" has remained steadfast. As laws were created to bring order and peace, lawyers were there to ensure their enforceability. Therefore, remember this history when others seek your advice or representation in a dispute and use it as a basis from which to incorporate the other four principles discussed in the next chapters. You will be well on your way to the positive practice of law.

Some things can't be found in books.

CHAPTER TWO

Competency

There's a lot more to competence than a law degree and a modicum of courtroom skill.

~ Fred Thompson

The second principle to the positive practice of law is competency. Not so much in the sense of legal intellect, but rather the idea of exercising this intellect in the right context. Most, if not all, professional rules of conduct require a lawyer to be competent. This means the lawyer must demonstrate sufficient knowledge and proficiency in the analysis of precedent, use of legal principles, evaluation of evidence, and oral and written communication skills when engaged in representation. Naturally, the ability to exercise these skills effectively requires training and intelligence. In fact, we tend to think of the term "competence" as synonymous with intelligence. However, competence - in the broader sense - is really just the ability to perform a specific task, action or function successfully. The ability to perform successfully as a lawyer requires more than just knowing the law – it requires knowing yourself and knowing when practicality is more effective than legality.

Establishing competency begins with self-awareness. No doubt law school and work experience provide the best opportunities to achieve the necessary skills to practice law. However, in order to exercise these skills effectively, you must intimately know your personality, talents, and limitations. Practicing in an area of law that is in sync with your personality and utilizes your gifts better serves your clients, your colleagues and, more importantly, your well being, which is the crux of the positive practice of law.

What is your calling? Start by determining what activities you are exceptionally good at doing and what topics awaken your passion, creativity, and sense of fulfillment. Perhaps you have a passion for the environment, or criminal or social justice. Or, maybe you have an interest in family issues, property disputes, or malpractice. These questions are really best explored while you are in law school or during your first year of practice. However, if you are further along in your career, you can still redirect your focus.

Additionally, each one of us is born with a particular skill, talent, or personality trait that allows us to fulfill our passion in a positive way. For instance, you may have a calm sounding voice and be goal-oriented. These are qualities that could be beneficial in dispute resolution such as negotiation or mediation. Or, you may have a methodical approach to detail and a memory like an elephant, which could be beneficial in complex litigation or arbitration. On the other hand, you may possess an authoritative presence to which people positively respond; this could be useful in trial advocacy. Remember, the lawyer's primary role in society is to be "the peacemaker." You must determine the best way to fulfill this role.

Focusing on activities that interest you is critical: If you enjoy public speaking, then you may find some type of oral advocacy fulfilling. On the other hand, if researching and writing floats your boat, you may prefer a judicial clerkship or some kind of transactional work. The basic message here is to practice a type of law that fits your personality and utilizes your talents, and not what just offers a higher salary. Nothing will put you on a track to depression faster than working in an area of law for which you do not possess the talent, skill or interest.

There will be times, however, when you will be given assignments that place you outside your comfort zone or that involve an area of law that is of no interest to you. In this instance, your ability to perform successfully will largely depend on how well you do your homework. Adequate preparation is a critical component of competency. It requires taking the time to educate yourself on the facts and the law governing those facts. Obviously, such preparation comes more naturally when you have "answered your calling," so to speak. However, in those times when you have to put your calling on hold, failure to do the requisite research will only make your job harder and cause unnecessary stress on you and others. Although most law schools teach basic researching skills and how to use the research for advocacy, there is something to be said for also understanding the consequences of poor research beyond the risk of losing your argument. A court pleading or demand letter that cites wrong or outdated authority in support of an invalid argument patently undermines effective advocacy. Instead of addressing the issue and ascertaining a solution, your opponent, and potentially the judge, now must spend valuable time addressing your errors. Thoroughly researching any statutes, rules, regulations, ordinances, and case law pertaining to your issue *prior* to conveying any communication is crucial to practicing law positively. A competent lawyer takes the time to analyze the factual and legal elements of the problem and then thoroughly researches the rules and procedures that are available to solve it.

In addition to ensuring that your practice is the right fit, and that you are adequately prepared when it is not, you must also make sure that you maintain the right attitude. To be an effective peacemaker, you must possess the ability to detach yourself emotionally from your case and maintain objectivity. That is not to say withhold all care and compassion, but if you internalize your client's problem, a judge's ruling, or opposing counsel's poor behavior, your ability to perform your task as peacemaker will be severely compromised. Facts become distorted and communications turn hostile. As a counselor, you have a responsibility to maintain level-headedness no matter how heated the issues become. There is a difference between being passionate about a cause and overreacting to disagreement. The latter only leads to the negative practice of law.

Last, but certainly not least, competency also commands a healthy dose of practical thinking. Even if you graduated with top honors at your law school, you will not succeed if you lack basic common sense. Common sense is defined as the exercise of sound judgment without reliance on esoteric knowledge, study, or research. Let's say you are working on a case where it is clear from your research that the facts and law are on your side. However, enforcement of the issue will most certainly prolong the matter and may ultimately be financially detrimental to your client or have a prejudicial effect on the opposing party. Do you proceed with enforcement anyway, accomplishing nothing more than establishing that you were right, or do you entertain an alternative solution that moves the matter forward in a positive direction for everyone? Indeed, your objective should always be to reach the solution that makes the most sense under the circumstances. But, sometimes determining what makes the most sense requires a more practical approach as opposed to a strictly legal approach. You will find that in most cases the path of least resistance is usually the wiser choice. Remember that your client will most likely not see the forest for the trees. Your task is to show them the forest.

The rules of professional conduct and ethics require the lawyer to provide *competent* representation, which requires sufficient knowledge of legal principles and proficiency in certain skills. However, this requisite knowledge and proficiency is only effective if it is exercised in the context of who you are, with the right attitude, and within the parameters of common sense. Competency is more than just having a law degree; it is having a degree of personal knowledge that enables you to best utilize your law degree.

"Well, they say that less is more. I'm faultless, sinless, blameless and flawless!"

CHAPTER THREE

Humility

A man wrapped up in himself makes a very small bundle.

~ Benjamin Franklin

The positive practice of law begins with good relationships. And good relationships require a component of humility. Humility is not so much a character trait as it is a perspective. Once you begin experiencing your legal career through a humble lens, you will soon realize what a valuable asset humility can be.

Humility is often given a negative connotation, synonymous with timidity or lack of self-confidence. Actually, humility is seen as one of the highest of virtues and thus is routinely the aspiration of many religions and spiritual philosophies. Humility comes from the word "humus," which means "the earth." Humility is the idea of being grounded in the reality of who you are. It is maintaining self-confidence in affirming your own value without being boastful about your accomplishments or diminishing those of others. Essentially, it is the willingness to redirect your ego away from yourself to the larger goal of serving others. The humble lawyer understands that he is "just as valuable, and just as weak, as the people he is called" to counsel. (Chapman, 116).

This means letting go of the ego that was so carefully cultivated in law school. The inflated ego that may have served you well in law school will do you great harm in practice. To truly reap the benefits of practicing law with humility, you must first understand and accept that your law degree and law license only establish your right to practice law. These accomplishments do not mean that you are better than anyone else or that you are due more respect than others. So how do you maintain the self-confidence necessary to be a successful lawyer without sabotaging your career?

First, you have to understand the difference between true pride and false pride. True pride is having a sense of self-confidence without self-absorption. You acknowledge your abilities and recognize your limitations without the need for confirmation or approval from external sources. False pride, on the other hand, is the desire to exaggerate your abilities and disavow your limitations. This kind of pride relies on confirmation and approval from external sources to suppress the inner feeling of incompetence. In other words, your feelings of self-respect do not come from within, but instead depend solely on outside approval.

A product of false pride is arrogance – the act of pretending to be superior to others. The arrogant lawyer does not communicate difficult concepts in a simple and understandable manner, but instead uses fancy words to impress his client and appear smarter than his opponent. This feeling of superiority also breeds a false sense of entitlement. The arrogant lawyer drafts his client's bills in such a way that provides little information about the quality or quantity of the work done because the lawyer believes he is entitled to payment. It is easy to see how practicing law with a sense of false pride will quickly, and sometimes permanently, close doors to new opportunities, friendships, and inner peace. Humility is the product of true pride. A person with true pride is not concerned with whether they are superior to others, and instead focuses on how best to resolve an issue rather than how he looks while resolving it. As the co-founder of Hewlett-Packard, David Packard, once stated, "You shouldn't gloat about anything you've done; you ought to keep going and find something better to do."

When you practice law with humility, you believe that all people, including your client and opposing counsel, have inherent value. Gary Chapman, author of *Love as a Way of Life: Seven Keys to Transforming Every Aspect of Your Life*, says that when you perceive the value of others you are more inclined to see potential friendships with others. As a result, you will engage in more positive behavior by being courteous, cooperative and considerate. Humility is the foundation of human relationships, so only when you relate well to others in your practice of law can you practice law well.

However, the idea of practicing law with a perspective of humility presents several quandaries. First, there is an inherent conflict between servanthood and the lawyer's obligation to maintain objectivity. Servanthood is cultivated through humility, because in humility is an innate desire to care for and serve others. The legal profession includes service to others. In fact, the profession is arguably rooted in servanthood, because early speechwriters and advocates initially received no monetary compensation for their services. However, to become a true servant requires a kind of intimacy that is often avoided in the legal profession. Lawyers are led to believe that objectivity requires complete emotional separation from the client. Indeed, providing legal counsel in an objective manner is very important, as discussed in the previous chapter. However, this perceived need for emotional separation conflicts with the requisite emotional connection for servanthood. Therefore, you need to strike a careful balance between the two concepts where you maintain some level of an emotional connection with your client to value his or her needs, but still fulfill your responsibility to advise your client in an objective manner. As Atticus Finch told his daughter Scout, "You never really understand a person until you consider things from his point of view...until you climb inside of his skin and walk around in it." (Lee, 33).

Another quandary presented by the humble practice of law is the conflict between sacrificing one's ego for the greater good and

19

the duty of zealous representation. It is believed by some legal scholars that lawyers have "a personal moral obligation not to let a lawsuit degenerate into bitterness and revenge." (Osler, 10). To fulfill this obligation is to see value in not only the client, but in the opponent as well. As previously stated, the act of setting aside your own ego to affirm the value of others naturally leads to positive behavior such as courtesy and cooperation. However, this behavior seems directly opposite from the "winning at any cost" mentality believed to be required for zealous representation. It is important to remember that representing one's position with zeal just means doing so with enthusiasm, passion, and commitment - each of which are not negative concepts when performed in a humble context. Therefore, one should be able to zealously represent his client's position while maintaining his objective toward the greater good – cultivating good relationships with opponents and seeing the process of litigation as a method of dispute resolution, instead of as an opportunity to exhibit false pride.

The final quandary is the recognition of your limitations versus the expectation of perfection. The humble lawyer acknowledges and accepts that he or she does not know, and will not know, everything about the law. (The phrase "I'll get back to you" is invaluable). There will be plenty of times in your journey as a lawyer when you will be in a situation of not having all of the answers. It is not beneath the humble lawyer to reach out to colleagues for help, because that lawyer sees the value of the colleague's assistance. In addition, the sense of humility brings with it the understanding that obstacles may arise that are out of your control. Therefore, the humble lawyer accepts failures and setbacks, and is quietly confident in her ability to find alternative solutions.

In spite of this, there is the belief that the failure to solve a problem or admitting that you don't know the answer indicates weakness. Some believe that because lawyers have a responsibility to the law, getting the law right is a legitimate expectation. But getting it right doesn't always mean getting it perfect. What is important to remember here is that you are *practicing* the law. You are practicing it so that you may know it and become better at it. Striving for perfection in every task will most certainly stifle any creativity because the fear of failure will prevent you from trying new strategies or a new practice. If you valued your client in your service to them, treated others with respect, and maintained good relationships along the way, then you did your job perfectly regardless of the outcome.

Humility does not come easily, but it is a worthy and attainable goal in your practice. In law school, you were taught to judge yourself in comparison with your classmates. Sometimes feeling superior to others seemed like the only way to survive. Now that you have obtained the right to practice law, doing it humbly is essential to your professional survival. So remember, when in an argument, do not cut the other person off or raise your voice to drown them out. Sometimes the best strategy is to just stop talking and let the other person be heard. When communicating difficult concepts, speak to others in simple and understandable terms. When sending a bill to a client, provide a short but clear narrative of the work done. Finally, when you are stumped on a problem, ask someone for help.

In the competitive culture of the legal profession, the idea of being self-effacing is a difficult one to grasp. However, the liberation that humility offers will bring inner peace and allow you to invest your time and energy in relationships with others, which is the key to success in your career. As one wise lawyer once stated, "Never underestimate the power of a kind word. Never underestimate our ability to do good." (Weidner, 20).

*"Psst!...do it man...bill for that two hour lunch you had with your mother...you did **think** about your client during lunch, right?"*

CHAPTER FOUR

Integrity

The right to do something does not mean that doing it is right.

~William Safire

Integrity is always at the top of the list of personal qualities most critical to the positive practice of law. Basically, integrity means a firm adherence to a code of moral or ethical values in which thoughts, decisions, and actions conform to ethical principles. It is, in essence, principle-centered living, or stated another way, doing what is right rather than what is convenient - a prized quality in life and fundamental to the practice of law. Atticus Finch's representation of a black man in the segregated South during the depression has served as a model of integrity for lawyers for many years. Another great example of integrity comes from the life of Bobby Jones.

Jones was a lawyer and an accomplished golfer, being the first to achieve the Grand Slam, winning four major tournaments in a single year and 13 championships from 1923 through 1930. During one national championship, he drove his ball into the woods and then accidentally nudged it. Although no one saw him move the ball, he penalized himself one stroke, which caused him to lose the game by that margin. When praised for his integrity, he said, "You might as well praise a man for not robbing a bank."

Like humility, integrity is empowering and freeing because you are doing what you believe is right regardless of the outcome. The liberation that integrity offers is why it is a key principle in the positive practice of law. Many respectful sources, including Jiminy

Cricket, tell us that living a life that is consistently true to one's conscience is a direct path to satisfaction. So naturally, when the conscience is ignored, the potential for satisfaction is severely undermined. This is especially valid in the legal profession where the overall objective is to uncover the truth. Once that truth is revealed, the lawyer can choose to either work within the parameters of that truth (take actions that reflect core values) or distort that truth (ignore those values). Which direction you take can depend on your focus.

Young lawyers have a tendency to focus on acquiring those material things which are perceived to symbolize or suggest prestige, power, or affluence. While this goal is arguably sought by most hardworking professionals, problems arise when one sacrifices his own personal values and conscience in the pursuit of this goal. This sacrifice may be driven by the desire for financial wealth and the affluent lifestyle seemingly enjoyed by partners and more senior colleagues, or by the need for affirmation from clients, colleagues, and judges. No matter what the driving force may be, it is important to understand that such a sacrifice of self contributes to professional negativity and dissatisfaction. That is not to say that symbols of success and conscience-driven decision making could not exist simultaneously. But, only the latter can provide a sense of fulfillment in having done your part honorably and completely. This sense of fulfillment will ultimately improve your ability to accept a negative outcome more easily rather than viewing it as a loss or failure.

Integrity is a developed skill that is perhaps best practiced in the legal profession where opportunities to do right seem endless. It is easy to lose your way, however, especially in a failing economy where the temptation to distort the truth may be prevalent. It can start with a deceptively small compromise or rationalization that, over time, becomes easier to grow larger. To maintain integrity, you should base all decisions or actions that rely on truth and honesty, no matter how insignificant, on your core values. A habit of constant reference to your conscience will result in actions that intuitively reflect yourself, and thus provide you with an enduring sense of satisfaction. Indeed, integrity does not provide instant gratification. In some instances, the benefits of integrity may not be seen for quite some time. If you recall from the example, no one saw Bobby Jones penalize himself one stroke for accidentally nudging the ball. However, a consistent practice of decision-making guided by integrity will yield positive rewards: You will experience growth in self-confidence and courage, respect from colleagues, and your employer will place more trust in you and your abilities.

Indeed, integrity takes courage for it requires doing the right thing even in the worst of circumstances. But, as pointed out in an October 2007 article for the American Bar Association's Law Practice Today titled "Living With Integrity," integrity also requires no defense:

> Integrity is one of those intangibles which can affect us in very tangible ways. It is also one of the only things we can possess which cannot be taken from us without our consent. People can have the power to take our wealth, health, objects of desire, and even our ideas. But they cannot take our integrity without our willing consent. And most things of importance in our lives must be defended. But integrity needs no defense. No one has to make an excuse for being truthful and honest in all regards.

As a famous lawyer named Abraham Lincoln once said, "resolve to be honest in all events," and you can rest assured your professional life will take care of itself.

"*Congratulations! Here is your settlement money. Now about my fee...*"

CHAPTER FIVE

Credibility

The more you are willing to accept responsibility for your actions,
the more credibility you will have.

~ **Brian Koslow**

A wise person once said, "Credibility is like virginity. Once you lose it, you can never get it back." And in the law, once it's lost you might as well hand over your license and bar card. Credibility is the bedrock of the positive practice of law. But what is *credibility* exactly? Basically, it is the ability to elicit, convey, and maintain believability. This ability begins with two key components: Trust and expertise.

Trust is the cornerstone of credibility. In order for someone to believe you, they need to trust you. Most legal disputes are in essence a breakdown in trust. Thus, restoring trust is fundamental to resolving the dispute. Consequently, it is imperative that those tasked with resolving the dispute, i.e. the lawyers, be vigilant about establishing and maintaining trust in their dealings with others. Whether a person can be deemed credible is often a subjective determination, because it usually refers to someone's reputation for truthfulness. Therefore, in a world where lawyers have been thought of as untrustworthy for centuries, a reputation for trustworthiness can go a long way. The other component, expertise, essentially requires you to be a good source of information and help for others. Although both components are established over time, it is important to demonstrate both qualities right out of the gate to the extent possible.

The reason why credibility is imperative to a positive law practice is simple: it makes the lawyer more likeable. People prefer to do business with other people who are similar to them. We are not perfect; therefore, we don't like other people who pretend to be perfect. Being honest about your limitations is one way people can identify with you. This level of candor makes others feel that you will be honest in your dealings with them. As a result, they are more likely to open up to you, which in turn presents an opportunity for you to learn more. As previously stated, admitting weaknesses in an extremely competitive profession can be difficult to do. There will be moments when you will be tempted to cover up your weaknesses and act overconfident. Yet, according to research by Barbara Spellman, a Professor of Psychology at the University of Virginia, people who come across as arrogant and overconfident are actually less believable than people who are unsure of themselves. Therefore, do not hesitate to inform others of what you know, what you can do, and what you need to do in order to do what is being asked of you. People appreciate forthrightness. Such candor can bring great rewards.

Likeability also gives you the power to influence. As you build your reputation of trust, you become more likeable by others, which helps cultivate your ability to persuade and influence. Eventually, others will view you as the "go-to" person for information or insight on a particular issue, which develops into expertise. The ultimate reward is more opportunities to serve those you were called to counsel.

But how does one establish credibility? There are numerous ways, most of which may sound insignificant, but remember even the smallest act of trust adds another building block to your reputation as a credible lawyer. Your goal is to always make deposits into your "trust" account, never withdrawals. Consistency in your actions and behavior is the keystone to building a credible reputation.

One important way you can establish credibility is to always do what you say and do not cut corners doing it. If you cannot be trusted to get something done, you are sending all sorts of negative messages to others. Get the job done the way it should be done. A classic example is failing to update your research. If your assignment is to research a particular issue and you find a court case on point, but fail to check that it has not been overturned or disapproved by another court, you risk losing not only your argument, but also your credibility as a lawyer. The lawyers who carry out assignments in an earnest and thorough manner are the ones who are most likely to get future work.

Other simple ways to establish and build your credibility include sincere listening and good communication. Learn all you can about the client, the client's problem, and how the client wants to solve the problem. This requires *real* listening: That means putting the Blackberry away and giving that person your undivided attention. Attentive listening results in solid legal analysis. Also, good communication is important when explaining your analysis to your client and others. Conveying the information in simple terms - not legalese - shows respect for the person on the receiving end and demonstrates your desire for them to accurately and clearly understand how you can help them.

Credibility is the foundation from which a successful legal career is built. Therefore, the loss of credibility will inevitably end your legal career. One sure way to lose credibility is lying to others. This includes fudging, whether it be by overstating the facts in a case, misrepresenting the holding in a case, or misstating the position of the opposing party. Stretching or shading the truth is not zealous representation, but mendacious representation. Also, as an advisor, you are expected to be forthcoming with any significant and impactful information. Notwithstanding strategic decisions to delay the release of information which is often customary in litigation, consistently holding back information or keeping silent when you are expected to raise awareness of certain information can be construed as lying. Once a reputation for lying is established, your ability to be an effective advocate for others will be severely compromised. Simply stated, good lawyers do not lie.

Another way to undermine your credibility is unprofessional behavior, such as overreacting in a courtroom to testimony, a ruling, or an objection with which you don't agree. Such matters should not be taken personally. This internalization not only reflects negatively on your competency but damages credibility as well. Also, belittling or mistreating staff or opposing counsel can impair your ability to establish relationships. Treating an opponent and others with respect and professional courtesy creates an amiable rapport that bestows credibility and influence.

Credibility is one of the most important qualities for a positive legal career. You cannot exude influence or persuade others if they do not believe the sincerity of your words, actions, and motives. Having a reputation as a credible lawyer will open doors and provide many opportunities for you to serve and make a real difference in the lives of others – which is at the heart of the positive practice of law.

CONCLUSION

The objective of the practice of law is to uncover the truth. The objective of the *positive* practice of law is to uncover the truth about you. It is about staying true to your core values and acting with consistency within the parameters of those values. It is about staying true to your personality and gifts without being boastful or self-important about your gifts. It is about building your reputation and building relationships while providing a valuable service to others. Finally, it is about knowing where you came from and aspiring to do better where you are going. If you apply these five principles to your practice of law, your experience and career will be nothing less than a positive one.

Bibliography

Books

Andrus, R. Blain. (2009). *Lawyer: A Brief 5,000 Year History.* Chicago, Illinois: American Bar Association.

Chapman, Gary. (2008). *Love As a Way of Life: Seven Keys to Transforming Every Aspect of Your Life.* Colorado Springs, Colorado: Waterbrook Press.

Friedman, Lawrence M. (2005). *A History of American Law.* 3rd Ed. Portland, Oregon: Book News, Inc.

Lee, Harper. (1960, renewed 1988, 2010 50th Anniversary Ed.). *To Kill A Mockingbird.* New York, New York: HarperCollins Publishers.

Kinnane, Charles H. (1952). *Anglo American Law.* 2nd Ed., Indianapolis, Indiana: The Bobb-Merrill Company, Inc.

Wolpert, Daniel. (2003). *Creating a Life with God: The Call of Ancient Prayer Practices.* Nashville, Tennessee: UpperRoom Books.

Journals/Articles

MacQueen, Kim. (2008, May). FLA Handling More Mental Health Calls. *The Florida Bar News*, 35(9).

McElhaney, Jim. (2010, Jan). The Power of Plain Talk. *ABA Journal*. 22-23.

Weidner, Donald J. (2004, March). The Common Quest for Professionalism. *The Florida Bar Journal.* LXXVIII(3), 18-22.

Electronic Journals/Articles/Book Excerpts

Barnes, Harrison A. Credibility and Your Legal Career. *General Counsel Consulting.* Retrieved from http://www.gcconsulting.com/articles/120007/62.

C.C. (2009, Sept.). Depression in the Legal Profession: Lawyers are the Most Likely to be Depressed. *Law Vibe.* Retrieved from http://lawvibe.com/depression-in-the-legal-profession-lawyers-are-the-most-likely-to-be-depressed.

Dayhoff, Signe. (2010, Feb.). What Do Individual Lawyers Need? Ways to Increase Their Credibility. *Ezine Articles.* Retrieved from http://ezinearticles.com.

Freeman, Ellen. (2007, Oct.) Living With Integrity. *Law Practice Today.* Retrieved from www.abanet.org/lpm/lpt/articles/mgt10072.shtml.

Gallozzi, Chuck. Examples of Integrity. *Personal Development.* Retrieved from http://www.personal-development.com/chuck/integrity.htm.

Golson, Hodges. The Laws of Influence. *MPG Management Psychology Group.* Retrieved from http://www.managementpsychology.com.

Hidalgo, Chris C. (2002, Dec.). Definition of Integrity. Retrieved from http://www.webweevers.com/integrity.htm.

Jones, Don P. & Crowley, Michael J. (2010). "I Wish I Would Have Called You Before…": Depression and Suicide; Make Sure You Don't Utter Those Words. *American Bar Association.* Retrieved from http://www.abanet.org/barserv/barleader/22-6wish.html.

King, Serge K. (2005). Pride and Humility. *Aloha International.* Retrieved from http://www.huma.org.

Korol, Sara (2009, Nov.). Re-considering Credibility. *Baldy Center for Law & Social Policy.* Retrieved from http://baldycenter.wordpress.com.

Krieger, Lawrence S. (1998, Mar.). What We're Not Telling Law Students – And Lawyers – That They Really Need To Know. *Journal of Law and Health*, 13(1). Available at http://findarticles.com/p/articles/mi_hb3048/is_1_13/ai_n28722129/.

Ludwig, George. Leadership Demands Integrity by Example. Retrieved from www.frugalmarketing.com/dtb/integrity-by-example.shtml.

Osler, Mark W. (2008, Sept.). The Lawyer's Humble Walk. Pepperdine Law Review, Vol. 32, No. 483, 2005. Also, available at SSRN: http://ssrn.com/abstract=1263568.

Martinuzzi, Bruna. (2006). Humility – The Most Beautiful Word in the English Language. *Mind Tools.* Retrieved from http://www.mindtools.com.

Muir, Ronda. (2008, Sept.). The Depression Demon Coming Out of the Legal Closet. *Law People: Law Practice Management, Law Firm Coaching: Ronda Muir of Robin Rolfe Resources: Law People Blog.* Retrieved from http://www.lawpeopleblog.com/tags/lawyers-and-mental-illness/.

Norman, Nancy. (2003, Aug. 29). Humility A Key Trait. *Sun Sentinel.* Retrieved from http://articles.sun-sentinel.com.

O'Connor, Lona. (1998, July 20). A Bit of Humility Can Be A Valuable Career Aid. *Sun-Sentinel.* Retrieved from http://articles.sun-sentinel.com.

Policarpio, Rainer. (2007, Sept.) Being a Lawyer Involves Continuous Learning. *Amazine.* Retrieved from http://www.amazine.com.

Reynolds, Susan. (2009, April). The Emergence of Professional Law in the Long Twelfth Century. *Law and History Review*, Vol. 21, issue 2. Retrieved from http://www.historycooperative.org/journals/1hr/21.2/forum_reynolds.html.

Rowland, Cynthia. (2010, March). Humility, Part Two. *She Thinks*. Retrieved from http://womenlawyerleaders.blogspot.com.

Sabris, Christopher & Webert, Daniel. (2002). Understanding the "Knowledge" Requirement of Attorney Competence: A Roadmap for Novice Attorneys. *Georgetown Journal of Legal Ethics*. Retrieved from http://findarticles.com

Smith, Beverly G. (1998). The Lawyer as a Professional. *Professional Conduct for Judges and Lawyers Preview*. 3d. ed. Retrieved from http://www.mlb.nb.ca/site/Bookch1.htm.

Sushelsky, Maxine. (2010). Law Practice and its Relevance to Lawyer's Mental Health: Damages and Remedies. *Lawyers with Depression*. Retrieved from http://www.lawyerswithdepression.com/TheLawPractice.asp.

Suvor, Daniel, Carlton, Richard & Thibault, Janis. (2008, May). Depression Takes a Heavy Toll On Lawyers. *California Bar Journal*. Retrieved from http://www.calbar.ca.gov.

Sweeney, Michael J. (2008). The Devastation of Depression: Lawyers Are at Greater Risk – It's an impairment to take seriously. *American Bar Association*. Retrieved from http://www.abanet.org.

Ward, Raymond. (2006, Sept.). A Lawyer's Recipe for Depression. Retrieved from http://www.typepad.com/t/trackback/106264/5871032.

Weiss, Debra C. (2007, Dec.). Lawyer Depression Comes Out of the
Closet. *ABA Journal.* Retrieved from
http://www.abajournal.com/news.

Weiss, Debra C. (2009, Feb.). Perfectionism, 'Psychic Battering'
Among Reasons for Lawyer Depression. *ABA Journal.* Retrieved
from http://www.abajournal.com/news.

Websites

American Bar Association. (2006, April). *Problematic
Perfectionism.* Retrieved from
http://www.abajournal.com/magazine.

BusinessDictionary.com. *Competence.* Retrieved from
http://www.businessdictionary.com.

Golden Gate University. (2010). *Minimum Competency.* Retrieved
from http://www.ggu.edu.

Lawyers Wellbeing Blog. (2010, Feb.). *Humility, Relationship-
Building and Career Satisfaction.* Retrieved from
http://www.lawyerswellbeing.com

The Mississippi Bar Association. (2010, August). *MS Bar History.*
Retrieved from http://www.msbar.org/history.php.

The North Carolina Court System. *What Can Young Lawyers Do to
Enhance Professionalism?* Retrieved from
http://www.nccourts.org.

Oregon State Bar. (2007, Aug/Sept.). *Conduct Counts:
Professionalism for litigation and courtroom practice.* Retrieved
from http://www.osbar.org.

Office of Disciplinary Council of the Supreme Court of Delaware. (2003, Dec.). *Principles of Professionalism for Delaware Lawyers*. Retrieved from http://courts.delaware.gov.

US Legal. *Credibility Law & Legal Definition*. Retrieved from http://definitions.uslegal.com.

Wikipedia. *Bar Associations*. Retrieved from http://www.wikipedia.org/wiki/bar_association?wwparam=1283278321.

Wikipedia. *Credibility*. Retrieved from http://www.wikipedia.org/wiki/credibility.

Wikipedia. *History of the Legal Profession*. Retrieved from http://www.wikipedia.org/wiki/history_of_the_legal_profession.

Wikipedia. *Humility*. Retrieved from http://www.wikipedia.org/wiki/humility.

Wikipedia. *Law Schools in the United States*. Retrieved from http://www.wikipedia.org/wiki/law_schools_in_the_United_States.

Transcripts

Carrick, Damien & Barraud, Anita. (2008, March). *Law Report: Lawyers and Depression*. Retrieved from http://www.abc.net.au/rn/lawreport/stories/2008/2195243.html.

Legal

Fla. R. Prof. Resp. 4-1.1. Competence.